His Dwelling Place

PHYSIOLOGY OF DISEASE

Is there a connection between behavior, attitudes, thoughts, emotions, feelings, beliefs and disease?

Acknowledgment

We are very grateful to Dr. Art Mathias, founder of Wellspring Ministries, for allowing us to include quotes, concepts and teachings from his books "Biblical Foundations of Freedom," "In His Own Image" and "The Continuing Works of Christ.

All Scripture quotations are taken from the New King James Version™.
Copyright © 1982 by Thomas Nelson, Inc.
Used by permission. All rights reserved.

His Dwelling Place Ministries
1835A Centre City Pkwy
Box # 416
Escondido, California 92025
858-618-5463
www.hisdwellingplace.com

Table of Contents

Physiology of Disease

Physiology of Disease

I. The Way Things Work

A. Is there a connection between behavior, attitudes, thoughts, emotions, feelings, beliefs and disease?

1. Hippocrates (the Father of Medicine) in 500 B.C. believed thought was linked with disease.

2. In the Garden, God connected man's thoughts and choices with death.

   - *"...but of the tree of Knowledge of Good and Evil, you shall not eat, for in the day that you eat of it, you shall surely die."* **Genesis 2:17**

3. Around 1500 B.C., Moses confirmed that God had not changed His mind. God graphically explains the connection between our choices and their consequences.

   - *"I have set before you life and death, blessing and cursing; therefore choose life, that both you and your descendants may live; that you may love the Lord your God, that you may obey His voice, that you may cling to him, for He is your Life and the length of your days."* **Deuteronomy 30:19-20**

       - Obedience to God = Life / Blessings / Health
           = Deut. 28:1-14 — Blessings
       - Obedience to Satan = Death / Curses / Disease
           = Deut. 28:15-68 — Curses

   - *"The thief does not come except to steal, and to **kill**, and to destroy. I have come that they may have **life**, and that they may have it more abundantly."* **John 10:10**

B. Do WORDS Matter?

1. "Sticks and stones will break my bones, but **WORDS** will never hurt me."

   "Death and life are in the power of the tongue, and those who love it will eat its fruit."
   Proverbs 18:21

2. God used **WORDS** to create the universe.

   *"And God **said**, 'Let there be light.'"* **Genesis 1:3**

Our thoughts consist of **WORDS.**

"As a man thinks in his heart, so is he." **Proverbs 23:7**

"Jesus said….'Either make the tree good and its fruit good, or else make the tree bad and its fruit bad; for a tree is known by its fruit. Brood of vipers! How can you, being evil, speak good things? For out of the abundance of the heart the mouth speaks **(WORDS)**. *A good man out of the good treasure of his heart brings forth good things, and an evil man out of the evil treasure brings forth evil things.* **But I say to you that for every idle WORD men may speak, they will give account of it in the day of judgment. For by your WORDS you will be justified, and by your WORDS you will be condemned.'"***
Matthew 12:33-37

"In the beginning was the **WORD.***"* **John 1:1**

"Pleasant **WORDS** *are as a honeycomb, sweet to the soul and health to the bones."*
Proverbs 16:24

"Jesus said, '…hear and understand: Not what goes into the mouth defiles a man: but what comes out of the mouth **(WORDS)**, *this defiles a man.'"* **Matthew 15:10-11**

"Let your heart retain my **WORDS**, *keep my commands and live…do not forget, nor turn away from the* **WORDS** *of my mouth…take a firm hold of instruction, do not let go; keep her (wisdom), for she is your life…my son, give attention to my* **WORDS**; *incline your ear to my sayings…do not let them (My* **WORDS**) *depart from your eyes; keep them (My* **WORDS**) *in the midst of your heart; for they (My* **WORDS**) *are life to those who find them, and health to all their flesh."* **Proverbs. 4:4-5, 13, 20-23**

Two of many resources used for this teaching:

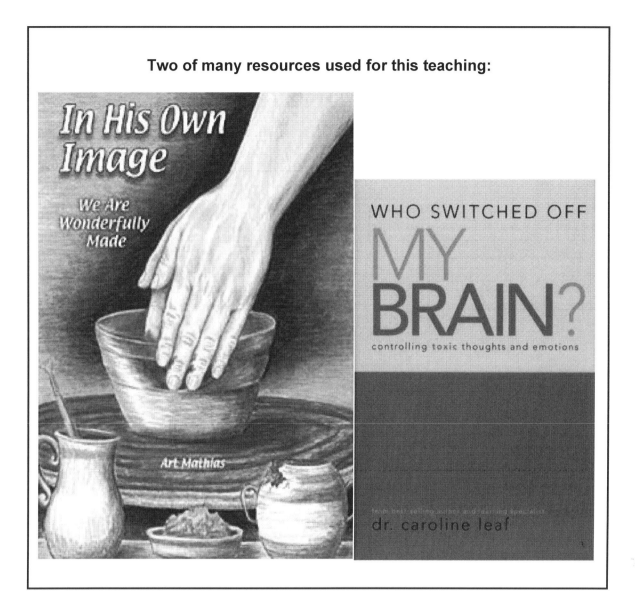

3. What is Disease?

    a. Definition: An abnormal condition of an organism or part, especially as a consequence of infection, inherent weakness or environmental stress, that impairs normal physiological function.

    b. <u>Dis</u>-ease = lack (invalidation, deprivation, reversal, removal, rejection) of **ease**.

II. <u>**The 11 Systems of the Body**</u>
    A. **Skeletal, Muscular, Circulatory, Respiratory, Digestive, Excretory, *Nervous (Limbic)*, *Endocrine*, Integumentary, Reproductive, *Immune***

The Limbic System
Electrical Messaging System

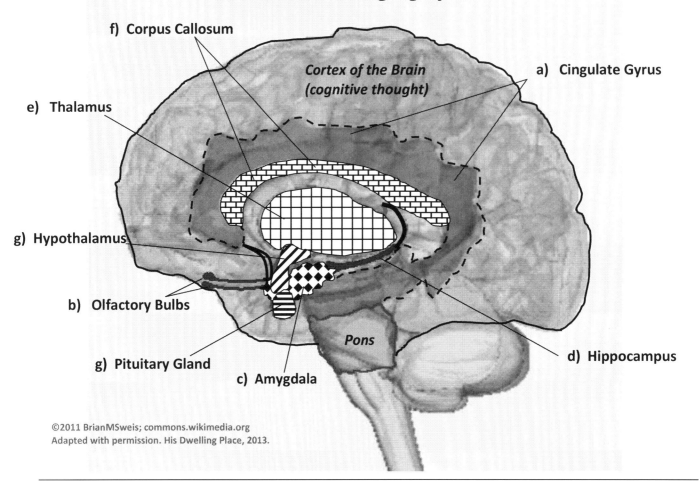

f) Corpus Callosum

Cortex of the Brain
(cognitive thought)

a) Cingulate Gyrus

e) Thalamus

g) Hypothalamus

b) Olfactory Bulbs

g) Pituitary Gland

c) Amygdala

Pons

d) Hippocampus

Nerve Cell

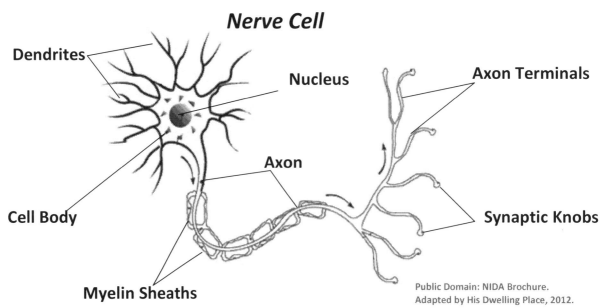

Dendrites

Nucleus

Axon Terminals

Axon

Cell Body

Synaptic Knobs

Myelin Sheaths

III. Three Systems at Work: Blessed / At Peace / In Balance

A. The Limbic System (Nervous System)
Classical conditioning = "Fired together, wired together"

1. Location: mid-brain ("emotional transit center")

2. Function: influences unconscious and instinctive behaviors, such as "fight or flight" and reproduction; integrates brain activity; involved in control of autonomic nervous system ("automatic," subconscious: heart rate, body temp, hunger signals, digestion, breathing); contributes to homeostasis (being at peace)

3. Organs:

   a. <u>Cingulate gyrus</u> — modifies behavior and emotions according to social and moral factors

   b. <u>Olfactory bulb (2)</u> — connects the sense of smell with the formation of memory and emotions

   c. <u>Amygdala (2)</u> — "library of the emotions;" central to the formation and storage of memories associated with emotional events; includes emotional reactions such as anger

   d. <u>Hippocampus (2)</u> — short-term memory; involves learning, accessing memory, recognition of novelty, recognition of spatial relationships

   e. <u>Thalamus</u> (part of the brain stem) — "air traffic controller;" interprets signals from Limbic system to regulate blood pressure, heart beat, respiration, digestion, swallowing, vomiting

   f. <u>Corpus Callosum</u> — analyzes and sorts information held in the hippocampus; seat of one's "free will"

   g. Limbic structure, in direct connection with the <u>hypothalamus and pituitary gland</u> (glands in the Endocrine system), are responsible for homeostasis

4. Neurotransmitters: chemical substances (hormones) that transmit information between nerve cells

   ◆ Essential for our discussion: adrenaline, nor-adrenaline, dopamine, ACH (acetylcholine), serotonin, GABA, etc.

The Endocrine System

Chemical Messaging System

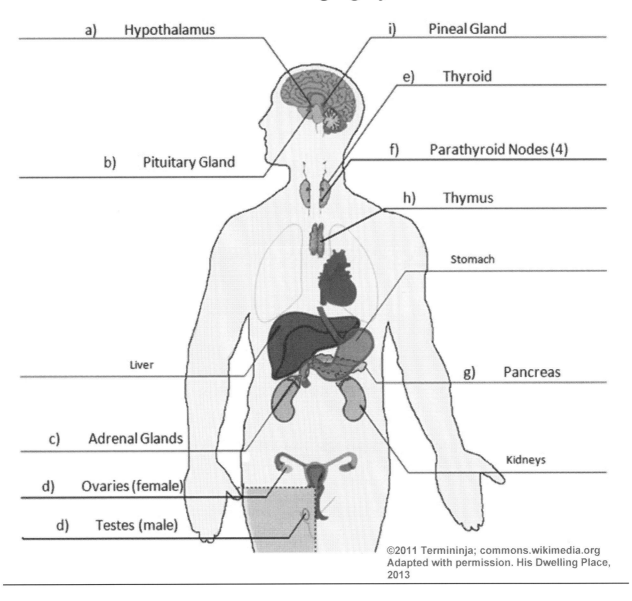

a) Hypothalamus

i) Pineal Gland

e) Thyroid

b) Pituitary Gland

f) Parathyroid Nodes (4)

h) Thymus

Stomach

Liver

g) Pancreas

c) Adrenal Glands

Kidneys

d) Ovaries (female)

d) Testes (male)

Notes:

B. The Endocrine System

1. Location: nine glands throughout the body (i.e., brain, throat, thorax)

2. Function: controls metabolism, water and mineral balance, sexual development, body's reaction to stress (in response to nervous system); transfers information throughout body; homeostasis

3. Glands:

   a. Hypothalamus — known as the "supervisor of the body;" communicates with Limbic system through neurotransmitters, triggers "fight or flight," also controls hunger and thirst, blood pressure, heart rate, body temp, sleep and wake cycle, sexual functions; produces releasing and inhibiting hormones

   b. Pituitary — stimulates other glands to produce hormones; tells adrenal gland to produce cortisol, the ovaries and testes to produce sex hormones, and the thyroid to release thyroxin; produces growth hormone (bones, organs, fat tissue and affects metabolism)

   c. Adrenal — produces cortisol, controls metabolism, reduces glucose intake in muscles and fat, protects body against stress, suppresses tissue inflammation, produces adrenaline and nor-adrenaline

   d. Sex Organs (Ovaries and Testes) — produces estrogen, progesterone, testosterone; stimulates cycles of reproduction

   e. Thyroid — produces thyroxin; controls metabolism (including heart rate and rate-of-energy use), lowers calcium levels in the blood

   f. Parathyroid — four small glands on the thyroid; increases blood calcium levels

   g. Pancreas — produces digestive enzymes, insulin (which lowers blood glucose levels and promotes energy storage), glucagons increases blood glucose

   h. Thymus — produces thymosin (stimulates maturing of T-cells)

   i. Pineal — produces melatonin (regulates the body clock, circadian rhythm), produces interleukin 2 (inhibits cancer)

The Immune System

Homeland Security

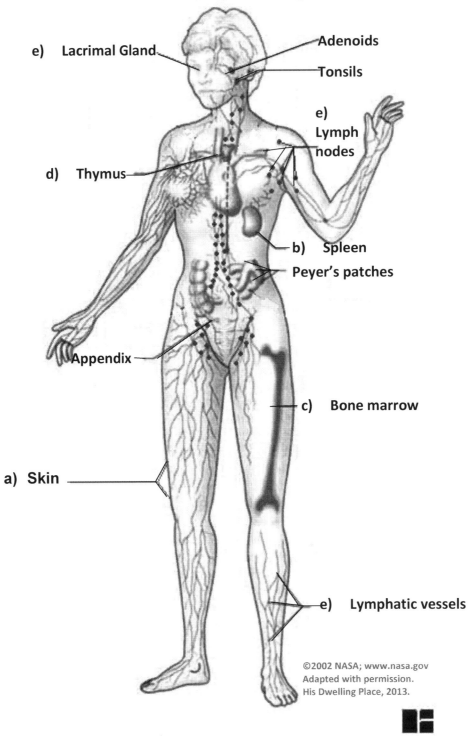

e)   Lacrimal Gland

Adenoids

Tonsils

e)
Lymph
nodes

d)   Thymus

b)   Spleen

Peyer's patches

Appendix

c)   Bone marrow

a) Skin

e)   Lymphatic vessels

©2002 NASA; www.nasa.gov
Adapted with permission.
His Dwelling Place, 2013.

14

C. The Immune System

1. Location: throughout the body

2. Function: to identify and destroy invaders/antigens (bacteria, viruses, fungi, tumors, parasites, cancers)

3. Components:

   a. Skin — exterior barrier against all foreign matter; largest organ of the body

   b. Spleen — matures lymphocytes

   c. Bone Marrow — produces lymphocytes (stem cells), white blood cells, macrophage/scavenger cells (ingests bacteria and dead cells)

   d. Thymus — matures stem cells to become T-cells; "school" of the immune system, "teaching" white blood cells to recognize self-tissue vs. invader

   e. Lymph System
      - Vessel System — no pump (heart), delivers and retrieves lymph from body tissue; movement of body "moves" lymph

      - Lymph — clear, watery fluid that contains white blood cells; removes invaders from tissue; supplies white blood cells to the blood/circulatory system

      - Lymph Nodes — glands that contain spaces where white blood cells and macrophages ingest foreign matter and debris; lymph is filtered from one node to the next, and then drains into the blood

   f. Lacrimal Glands — produce tears and protective enzymes

   g. Adenoids and Tonsils — produce antibodies against ingested or inhaled organisms

   h. White Blood Cells — branches of the military
      - T-Cells — killer cells that attack recognized invaders; mature in the thalamus

      - B-Cells — recognize antigens from former infections (i.e., childhood diseases, vaccinations, etc.)

      - Killer Cells — aggressive white cells that kill on contact; they put holes in the cell walls of viruses and cancers

      - Macrophage — help T-cells identify what they're supposed to kill

IV. **Fight or Flight, Stage One (The Alarm Reaction)** – *God-given response to danger, intended to save your life from natural disasters, intruders, accidents, etc.*

A. **The Endocrine System**

1. Awareness of danger puts the brain on alert, stimulating the hypothalamus to…

2. Trigger a "Jam Dive" (all hands on deck; go to emergency stations; no further instruction needed); immediate reaction to actual danger, then…

3. Adrenal Glands "dump" massive amounts of adrenaline and cortisol into the bloodstream, priming the body either to run away (quickly!) or face the danger:

4. Heart beats faster to move greater volume of blood, delivering chemical messages

5. Blood pressure rises

6. Pupils dilate for maximum light and vision

7. Hair stands on end; indicator of partial evacuation of blood from skin

8. Skin — if punctured, blood will quickly coagulate to prevent severe loss

9. Chest expands to increase volume of oxygen

10. Bronchials (pockets in lungs) relax, allowing greater volume of oxygen to enter the lungs

11. Muscles contract

12. Blood vessels near surface of skin contract, causing skin to turn pale; blood vessels constrict in non-essential systems (digestion, skin, peripheral muscles), to be redirected to "offensive" muscles (heart, legs, lungs)

13. Other blood vessels dilate; the liver releases glucose, which provides fuel for the muscles

14. Bladder and colon may release stored waste in extreme cases

B. **The Immune System**

1. Shuts down, along with the Digestive, Excretory and Reproductive systems — considered "unnecessary" to immediate survival

2. Blood diverts from existing injury, infection or diseased area to supply the energy for "fight or flight;" cortisol provides temporary anesthetic and anti-inflammatory effects

C. The Limbic System

1. Hypothalamus takes control of physical and emotional responses

2. Surrenders homeostasis for sake of survival

3. When danger is gone, Limbic System reinstates homeostasis with the assistance of the hypothalamus

V. <u>Fight or Flight, Stage Two (Stage of Resistance)</u> — *Misapplying the God-given response to danger by choosing **fear** over **faith** sets off "adrenaline-cortisol drip"*

A. The Limbic System — "Fired together, wired together"

1. **What we choose to do within the <u>first 60 seconds</u> of a stress encounter determines how our body will deal with that encounter**

2. A mechanism created to save your life, in the hands of the Enemy, will ***steal*** your peace, ***destroy*** your health, and — given enough time — ***kill*** you

3. "Toxic Thinking" (Dr. Caroline Leaf's term) poisons the body, like ingesting **arsenic** as a dietary supplement!

4. **Top Stressors — ways to give away your peace**

<u>Situation/Events</u>	<u>Demands</u>	<u>Physical</u>
Death of a loved one	Deadlines	Pregnancy
Catastrophic disaster	Competition	Surgery
Divorce or separation	Tests/exams	Loss of mobility
Relationship conflicts	Family/children problems	Feeling sick
Illness in a loved one	Financial pressures	Muscle aches/tension
Being sued	Too many responsibilities	Teeth grinding
Losing a job	Caring for others	Cold hands/cool feet
Job changes	Dieting	Rapid heartbeat
Retirement	Quitting smoking	High blood pressure
Financial loss	Public speaking	Nausea/diarrhea
Doctor appointments		Skin rashes
Dentist appointments	<u>Mood/Emotions</u>	Change in appetite
Failures/mistakes	Acute/chronic anxiety	Sleeping problems
Weddings	Anger	Sexual problems
Vacations	Frustration/impatience	Exhaustion/irritability
Holidays	Worry	Chronic illness
	Guilt/shame	
<u>Thoughts</u>	Depression/sadness	*(Most physical issues are*
Trouble concentrating	Resentment/hostility	*SYMPTOMS of Stage 2.*
Compulsive ruminating	Hopelessness	*Ironically, they **trigger***
Being overly critical	Powerlessness	*adrenaline/cortisol drip,*
Pessimism	Resignation/apathy	*causing more illness.)*

Fight or Flight Comparison Chart

Fight or Flight Stage I: "Appropriate Fear"	Fight or Flight Stage II: "Toxic Fear"
Hypothalamus starts adrenaline/cortisol surge: 1. **Heart rate** goes up 2. **Blood pressure** increases 3. **Blood pulled to body's core** for chemical/energy delivery 4. **Adrenaline circulation** to brain brings greater clarity and cognitive ability 5. **Eyes dilate** for better vision 6. **Glucose released** from storage for strength and endurance to fight or flee 7. **Muscles tense** for action 8. **Lungs expand** for greater breathing capacity 9. **Cortisol released** as temporary anti-inflammatory and pain-killer *Systems that shut down during "fight or flight" for the sake of survival; energy used elsewhere:* 1. <u>Immune System</u>: healing postponed 2. <u>Digestive System</u>: absorption stopped; stomach may empty (vomiting) 3. <u>Excretory System</u>: elimination stopped; bladder & colon may empty 4. <u>Reproductive System</u>: may induce early labor or skipped cycles	*Adrenaline and cortisol continue to "drip:"* 1. **Elevated heart rate**: cardiovascular diseases; dysrhythmia; heart failure 2. **High blood pressure**: (hypertension), strokes 3. **Poor circulation** in extremities; cold hands and feet 4. **Headaches**: light-headedness; brain fog; memory loss; insomnia; depression 5. **Eye strain**: retinal damage 6. **Altered blood sugar levels**: erratic metabolism; insulin suppressed by cortisol; lethargy; chronic fatigue 7. **Muscle spasms/cramps**: tension headaches; chronic back and neck pain 8. **Shortness of breath**: hyperventilation; fatigue; asthma 9. **Corrosive cortisol drip**: reduces ability to control inflammation; tissue repair slowed; aging accelerates *Systems that are suppressed during Fight or Flight Stage II:* 1. <u>Immune System</u>: healing slowed; low resistance to illness; recurring illness; allergies and chronic diseases develop 2. <u>Digestive System</u>: nausea; vomiting; indigestion; acid stomach; malabsorption; ulcers, Crohn's disease 3. <u>Excretory System</u>: incontinence; IBS; constipation; diarrhea; colitis; spastic colon 4. <u>Reproductive System</u>: infertility; irregular cycles; low sperm count; miscarriages

B. The Immune System

1. Production of white blood cells, stem cells, etc. slows:

    a. Fewer warriors are available to carry the same workload; the body is under-staffed and under-equipped

    b. But the enemies (antigens, viruses, bacteria) are still coming!

2. **Each <u>minute</u> of stress** suppresses the immune system for <u>21 hours</u>

3. **Allergies** develop as a result of taxing the immune system with stress

4. **Fear/Anxiety/Stress disorders** include the following:

Acne, ADD, bursitis, chronic fatigue syndrome, coronary disease, cystitis, cysts, depression, eclampsia, environmental illness, Epstein-Barr, erectile dysfunction, essential tremor, gallbladder disease, gastritis, gingivitis, hair loss, menopause aches, herpes/cold sores, infertility, iritis, kidney stones, phobias, postpartum depression, PMS, restless leg syndrome, sinusitis, ulcers, and more. *(**See Fight or Flight Stage II on opposite page.**)*

5. **Auto-immune diseases** are a result of <u>Stress</u> *compounded with* <u>Self-hatred</u>. *In other words, the immune system "turns on itself" and starts killing the body*

Addictions, amyotrophic lateral sclerosis, arthritis, Bell's palsy, carpal tunnel, celiac disease, chronic obstructive pulmonary disease, congestive heart failure, Crohn's disease, Cushing's syndrome, dementia, diabetes, eating disorders, fibromyalgia, glomerulonephritis, Graves/hyperthyroid, Guillain-Barre syndrome, Hashimoto's, HIV/AIDS, Hodgkin's disease, hyperparathyroidism, hypoglycemia, leaky gut, leukemia, Lewy body disease, lupus, Lyme disease, Meniere's disease, mononucleosis, multiple myeloma, myasthenia gravis, narcolepsy, multiple sclerosis, non-Hodgkin's lymphoma, osteoporosis, pericarditis, polycystic ovaries, psoriasis, pulmonary fibrosis, rheumatoid arthritis, synovitis, transient ischemic attacks, ulcerative colitis, uterine fibroids, vitiligo, and many more.

*"Peace I leave with you, My peace I give to you; NOT as the world gives do I give to you. Let not your heart be troubled, neither let it be afraid." **John 14:27***

DOES THIS LOOK LIKE PEACE TO YOU?

*"My people perish for lack of knowledge." **Hosea 4:6***

*"My people have gone into captivity because they have no knowledge." **Isaiah 5:13***

*"Anxiety in the heart of a man causes depression." **Proverbs 12:25***

C. The Endocrine System

1. Toxic effects of excess adrenaline and cortisol include:

   a. Gastric ulcers, excess stomach secretion

   b. Skin disorders — vitiligo (loss of pigmentation; white blotches)

   c. High blood pressure

   d. High cholesterol — plaque in arteries

   e. Panic disorders, "panic attacks"

   f. Heart and circulatory system damage — the most serious effect of persistent, elevated adrenaline (heart dysrhythmias, mitral valve prolapse)

   g. Suppression of immune system

   h. Arthritis, gout

   i. Rheumatoid arthritis

   j. Cancer — killer cells (cells that attack cancer) are suppressed

   k. Diabetes — cortisol blocks insulin

   l. Infertility and miscarriage — reproductive process suppressed

   m. Memory loss — cortisol/adrenaline "fry" the dendrites (nerve receptors)

VI. <u>Fight or Flight, Stage Three (Exhaustion)</u> — *After months, years or decades of fear and anxiety, our bodies simply wear out and give up. The enemy has won.*

A. Multiple diseases develop; ability to resist any mental or physical attack is gone

   1. Mild stressors can cause anaphylactic shock (MCSEI — Multiple Chemical Sensitivity Environmental Intolerance = allergic to everything)

   2. Small triggers produce exaggerated increases of cortisol and adrenaline

   3. Heart and adrenal failure

      a. It can literally cause death

   "...men's hearts [will fail] them from fear and the expectation of those things which are coming..." Luke 21:26

VII. How to fix it

A. The Nine Rs (Pray these OUT LOUD):

1. **Recognize** — admit your sin
2. **Take Responsibility** — choose to fix it
3. **Repent** — change your thinking to line up with God
4. **Renounce** — announce again your alignment with God's contract
5. **Remove** — tell the enemy to get off your property
6. **Replace** — renew your mind with the Holy Spirit's truth
7. **Resist** — put on your armor and take your thoughts captive
8. **Restore** — help others with their walk-out
9. **Rejoice**! — no explanation needed

B. Choose this day whom you will serve…choose LIFE!

1. **Forgive** your enemies (and forgive yourself and God) and **repent** for your sins.
   a. Stop being a victim! YOUR choices result in positive OR negative fruit!

2. Actively bless God: it will heal you. (Psalm 103:1-3)

3. Take your thoughts captive: ask yourself, "Is this truth, or a lie from the enemy?" (2 Cor. 10:3-5)

4. Guard your heart: (What do you FEED your soul? What do you read? What do you watch? What do you listen to? Where do you go?) (Proverbs 4:23)
   a. EVEN the evening news

5. Transform your mind: (Rom. 12:2) Science calls this "neuroplasticity"

6. Put your trust in God: He's your hiding place, fortress, deliverer, refuge. (Psalm 91)

7. You can do all things through Christ, who strengthens you. (Phil. 4:13)

8. Submit to God, resist the devil *and he will flee from you*. (James 4:7-8)

9. Confess your sins, pray for each other, and you will be healed! (James 5:16)

10. Put on the whole Armor of God. (Eph. 6:12-17)

11. Use your mouth to speak LIFE to yourself and others! Align with what God says, not what the enemy says! Every word that comes out of your mouth is either LIFE *or* DEATH! (Proverbs 18:21)

12. *Take* your peace! (Phil. 4:6-7; John 14:27)

C. LAUGH!

"A merry heart doeth good like a medicine, but a broken spirit dries up the bones."
Proverbs 17:22

100-200 laughs per day equal 10 minutes of exercise!

VIII. CONCLUSION: THE PROMISE

A. This is a message from your Loving Father:

"Look, you are being held captive by My enemy. You have chosen to serve him, and have been given the best he has to offer: sickness, loneliness, brokenheartedness, imprisonment and despair. But you know what? I love you. And if you trust Me, I will give you the strength to escape captivity."

"For I know the thoughts that I think toward you, says the Lord, thoughts of peace and not of evil, to give you a future and a hope. Then you will call upon Me and go and pray to Me (you will **recognize**, take **responsibility** for, and **repent** of your sin; forgive Me, yourself and others; **renounce** your agreement with the enemy; **remove** the enemy from the throne of your life) *and I will listen to you. And you will seek Me and find Me, when you search for me with all your heart. I will be found by you, says the Lord, and I will bring you back from your captivity* (disease, trauma, loneliness, brokenheartedness)*."* ***Jeremiah 29:11-13***

IX. RESOURCES

➢ *In His Own Image.* Art Mathias. Wellspring Publishing.

➢ *Who Switched Off My Brain?* Caroline Leaf, Ph.D. Inprov, Ltd.

➢ *Merck Manual of Medical Information: Home Edition, The.* 2ⁿᵈ Edition. Simon & Schuster.

➢ *Anatomica.* Chryl Campbell, editor. Global Book Publishing.

Blessing Your Body

BLESSING YOUR BODY

Heavenly Father, in the name of the Lord Jesus Christ and by the power of Your Holy Spirit, I come in obedience to Your Word. You have commanded, "You shall love your neighbor as yourself." This law was so important that you repeated it six times in Your Word: (Lev. 19:18, Matt. 19:19 and 22:39, Rom. 13:9, Gal. 5:14 and James 2:8). The message of the Law and the Prophets is to love You first and then myself, so that I can love my neighbor. I have repented of my sin against You, against myself and against my neighbor. Now, I stand in Your presence and I speak blessing on my body as an act of obedience to Your Word. *(Lay your hands on each part of your body as you speak this blessing.)*

Body, just as I am under the authority of the Lord Jesus Christ, you are under my authority. I am a servant of the Most High God, and you are in my service. I am responsible to care for you, nourish you and protect you. I am commanded to love you. I bless you and I thank you for all you do for me.

Nervous System *(brain, spinal cord, nerves, etc.),* I bless you and I thank you for filtering all the messages and signals that come your way. I break agreement with confusion, and I put on the mind of Christ. I bless your pathways. I bless you with clear thinking. I bless you with the cleansing and renewing of the Word of God. I bless you with the freedom that truth brings. I bless your work of taking every thought captive in obedience to Christ. I bless you in the work you do to guard my heart. I bless your sensitivity to the voice of the Holy Spirit. Electrical and chemical components, submit to the design of God. I speak health and healing to you. I bless you with peace.

Endocrine System *(adrenals, pituitary, hypothalamus, thyroid, etc),* I bless you. I thank you for all you do for me. I speak health and healing to you. I give you permission to calm down and to come into the peace of homeostasis. Adrenal glands, I have overworked you. I have repented and canceled my contracts with the enemy, and now I bless you! I speak health to you. I tell you to line up with the will of God. I thank you for all you've done. Now, be at peace.

Circulatory System *(heart, vessels, blood, etc.),* without you, I cannot live. I thank you for pumping life, nourishment, healing, strength and cleansing throughout my body. I have taxed you with my sin, but you have served me well. I speak health and healing and rest over you. I bless you with the peace that passes all understanding. Refreshing be upon you.

Respiratory System *(lungs, etc.),* you are essential. You are wonderful. You provide me with oxygen to keep my body functioning, and you remove waste to keep me cleansed. Thank you for fueling my body with life. I bless you with maximum capacity, and I speak refreshing over you. I speak healing and protection from the fear and the diseases that want to overtake you. I bless you with the strength to power words of life, songs of praise, messages of hope and peace, and words of wisdom and strength, all authored by the Holy Spirit. I bless you.

Digestive and Excretory Systems *(esophagus, stomach, intestines, colon, etc.)*, I bless you. I appreciate all you do for me. I bless you with health and peace. I bless all your functions with efficiency in digestion, absorption and waste disposal. I bless you with cleansing and rest.

Immune System *(lymph nodes, vessels, white blood cells, etc.)*, thank you for guarding me from invasion. I bless you. I speak strength to you. I release you to identify foreign invaders and to protect my body from assault. I bless your efforts to repair and heal my body. I bless the preventative work you do. I bless the health of my marrow to produce stem cells. I bless the training of those cells to know my genetic code and their efficiency in destroying invaders. I command my system to stop destroying my tissue and to start rebuilding those sites that have been under "friendly fire." I bless you with peace and truth.

Skeletal and Muscular System *(muscles, bones, joints, etc.)*, thank you for holding me up and moving me around. I bless you for defining my stature and shape. I bless the image God designed on His drawing board, and I call it good! I bless my height. It is perfect. I bless my shape. It is precious in His sight. I love you enough to help improve that which I can fix, and to love and accept that which is unchangeable. I bless you and I love you.

Reproductive System, I repent for misusing and despising your function. Your role is to create new eternal beings that bring glory to God. I bless your presence in my body. I bless your cycle *(male or female)*. I bless every part of you, seen and unseen. I bless every tissue and hormone that work together in this system. I bless my femaleness/ maleness. I bless this part of God that is reflected in me. I am no accident. My gender is not an accident. I am the righteousness of God in Christ, whether son or daughter. I bless you.

Blessing for specific body parts *(Bless any tissue or specific part that has been deformed, injured, diseased, destroyed, removed, in chronic pain or hated and rejected by you. If you haven't repented for self-hatred, repent as you go.)* I bless you, _____. You are special. You have attempted to operate for me, but my sin has hindered you. I love you and accept you. You have not been the traitor. You have not abandoned me. I speak restoration and healing to you, body. I bless you in the name of Jesus Christ through the power of the Holy Spirit, for this is the will of the Father who made me and loves me and calls His design of me, "Very good."

Bless your countenance *(Look at your image in a mirror. This is the part of you everyone sees. If you can't stand to look at yourself and say, "I love you and God loves you!" then you won't believe it when someone else says it.)* I love you! I am so glad you were born! You are precious in God's sight — worthy of His love, and worthy of my love. Only YOU can be who God created you to be! I bless you!

Proverbs 17:22 "...a broken spirit (fear and self-hate) dries up the bones."

Proverbs 16:24 "Pleasant words are as a honeycomb, sweet the to soul and health to the bones."

Contract With God

Contract with God:

Blessings on Obedience
Deuteronomy 28:1-14

[1] "Now it shall come to pass, if you diligently obey the voice of the LORD your God, to observe carefully all His commandments which I command you today, that the LORD your God will set you high above all nations of the earth. [2] And all these blessings shall come upon you and overtake you, because you obey the voice of the LORD your God:

[3] "Blessed *shall* you *be* in the city, and blessed *shall* you *be* in the country.

[4] "Blessed *shall be* the fruit of your body, the produce of your ground and the increase of your herds, the increase of your cattle and the offspring of your flocks.

[5] "Blessed *shall be* your basket and your kneading bowl.

[6] "Blessed *shall* you *be* when you come in, and blessed *shall* you *be* when you go out.

[7] "The LORD will cause your enemies who rise against you to be defeated before your face; they shall come out against you one way and flee before you seven ways.

[8] "The LORD will command the blessing on you in your storehouses and in all to which you set your hand, and He will bless you in the land which the LORD your God is giving you.

[9] "The LORD will establish you as a holy people to Himself, just as He has sworn to you, if you keep the commandments of the LORD your God and walk in His ways. [10] Then all peoples of the earth shall see that you are called by the name of the LORD, and they shall be afraid of you. [11] And the LORD will grant you plenty of goods, in the fruit of your body, in the increase of your livestock, and in the produce of your ground, in the land of which the LORD swore to your fathers to give you. [12] The LORD will open to you His good treasure, the heavens, to give the rain to your land in its season, and to bless all the work of your hand. You shall lend to many nations, but you shall not borrow. [13] And the LORD will make you the head and not the tail; you shall be above only, and not be beneath, if you [4]heed the commandments of the LORD your God, which I command you today, and are careful to observe *them.* [14] So you shall not turn aside from any of the words which I command you this day, *to* the right or the left, to go after other gods to serve them.

List **strongholds** that I do not agree with anymore. I am free of these words, thoughts and actions, i.e., Spirits of Bitterness, Self-Bitterness, Fear, Anxiety, Rejection, Unloving, Occult, Trauma, Envy and Jealousy, Unbelief, Soul Ties, Generational Curses, Occultic Practices, etc. List them here.	Because I believe and do the will of God, I am blessed with His peace and I receive all of His **promises** for my life and all my generations. List them here.

Contract Payment Terms: <u>Paid in Full by Jesus Christ</u>

Signature: _____   Date: _____

Contract With Satan

Contract with Satan:

Curses on Disobedience
Deuteronomy 28:15-68

[15] "But it shall come to pass, if you do not obey the voice of the LORD your God, to observe carefully all His commandments and His statutes which I command you today, that all these curses will come upon you and overtake you:

[16] "Cursed *shall* you *be* in the city, and cursed *shall* you *be* in the country.

[17] "Cursed *shall be* your basket and your kneading bowl.

[18] "Cursed *shall be* the fruit of your body and the produce of your land, the increase of your cattle and the offspring of your flocks.

[19] "Cursed *shall* you *be* when you come in, and cursed *shall* you *be* when you go out.

[20] "The LORD will send on you cursing, confusion, and rebuke in all that you set your hand to do, until you are destroyed and until you perish quickly, because of the wickedness of your doings in which you have forsaken Me. [21] The LORD will make the plague cling to you until He has consumed you from the land which you are going to possess. [22] The LORD will strike you with consumption, with fever, with inflammation, with severe burning fever, with the sword, with scorching, and with mildew; they shall pursue you until you perish. [23] And your heavens which *are* over your head shall be bronze, and the earth which is under you *shall be* iron. [24] The LORD will change the rain of your land to powder and dust; from the heaven it shall come down on you until you are destroyed.

[25] "The LORD will cause you to be defeated before your enemies; you shall go out one way against them and flee seven ways before them; and you shall become troublesome to all the kingdoms of the earth. [26] Your carcasses shall be food for all the birds of the air and the beasts of the earth, and no one shall frighten *them* away. [27] The LORD will strike you with the boils of Egypt, with tumors, with the scab, and with the itch, from which you cannot be healed. [28] The LORD will strike you with madness and blindness and confusion of heart. [29] And you shall grope at noonday, as a blind man gropes in darkness; you shall not prosper in your ways; you shall be only oppressed and plundered continually, and no one shall save *you*.

[30] "You shall betroth a wife, but another man shall lie with her; you shall build a house, but you shall not dwell in it; you shall plant a vineyard, but shall not gather its grapes. [31] Your ox *shall be* slaughtered before your eyes, but you shall not eat of it; your donkey *shall be* violently taken away from before you, and shall not be restored to you; your sheep *shall be* given to your enemies, and you shall have no one to rescue *them*. [32] Your sons and your daughters *shall be* given to another people, and your eyes shall look and fail *with longing* for them all day long; and *there shall be* no strength in your hand. [33] A nation whom you have not known shall eat the fruit of your land and the produce of your labor, and you shall be only oppressed and crushed continually. [34] So you shall be driven mad because of the sight which your eyes see. [35] The LORD will strike you in the knees and on the legs with severe boils which cannot be healed, and from the sole of your foot to the top of your head.

[36] "The LORD will bring you and the king whom you set over you to a nation which neither you nor your fathers have known, and there you shall serve other gods—wood and stone. [37] And you shall become an astonishment, a proverb, and a byword among all nations where the LORD will drive you.

[38] "You shall carry much seed out to the field but gather little in, for the locust shall consume it. [39] You shall plant vineyards and tend *them,* but you shall neither drink *of* the wine nor gather the *grapes;* for the worms shall eat them. [40] You shall have olive trees throughout all your territory, but you shall not anoint *yourself* with the oil; for your olives shall drop off. [41] You shall beget sons and daughters, but they shall not be yours; for they shall go into captivity. [42] Locusts shall consume all your trees and the produce of your land.

[43] "The alien who *is* among you shall rise higher and higher above you, and you shall come down lower and lower. [44] He shall lend to you, but you shall not lend to him; he shall be the head, and you shall be the tail.

[45] "Moreover all these curses shall come upon you and pursue and overtake you, until you are destroyed, because you did not obey the voice of the LORD your God, to keep His commandments and His statutes which He commanded you. [46] And they shall be upon you for a sign and a wonder, and on your descendants forever.

[47] "Because you did not serve the LORD your God with joy and gladness of heart, for the abundance of everything, [48] therefore you shall serve your enemies, whom the LORD will send against you, in hunger, in thirst, in nakedness, and in need of everything; and He will put a yoke of iron on your neck until He has destroyed you. [49] The LORD will bring a nation against you from afar, from the end of the earth, *as swift* as the eagle flies, a nation whose language you will not understand, [50] a nation of fierce countenance, which does not respect the elderly nor show favor to the young. [51] And they shall eat the increase of your livestock and the produce of your land, until you are destroyed; they shall not leave you grain or new wine or oil, *or* the increase of your cattle or the offspring of your flocks, until they have destroyed you.

[52] "They shall besiege you at all your gates until your high and fortified walls, in which you trust, come down throughout all your land; and they shall besiege you at all your gates throughout all your land which the LORD your God has given you. [53] You shall eat the fruit of your own body, the flesh of your sons and your daughters whom the LORD your God has given you, in the siege and desperate straits in which your enemy shall distress you. [54] The sensitive and very refined man among you will be hostile toward his brother, toward the wife of his bosom, and toward the rest of his children whom he leaves behind, [55] so that he will not give any of them the flesh of his children whom he will eat, because he has nothing left in the siege and desperate straits in which your enemy shall distress you at all your gates. [56] The tender and delicate woman among you, who would not venture to set the sole of her foot on the ground because of her delicateness and sensitivity, will refuse to the husband of her bosom, and to her son and her daughter, [57] her placenta which comes out from between her feet and her children whom she bears; for she will eat them secretly for lack of everything in the siege and desperate straits in which your enemy shall distress you at all your gates.

[58] "If you do not carefully observe all the words of this law that are written in this book, that you may fear this glorious and awesome name, THE LORD YOUR GOD, [59] then the LORD will bring upon you and your descendants extraordinary plagues—great and prolonged plagues—and serious and prolonged sicknesses. [60] Moreover He will bring back on you all the diseases of Egypt, of which you were afraid, and they shall cling to you. [61] Also every sickness and every plague, which *is* not written in this Book of the Law, will the LORD bring upon you until you are destroyed. [62] You shall be left few in number, whereas you were as the stars of heaven in multitude, because you would not obey the voice of the LORD your God. [63] And it shall be, *that* just as the LORD rejoiced over you to do you good and multiply you, so the LORD will rejoice over you to destroy you and bring you to nothing; and you shall be plucked from off the land which you go to possess.

[64] "Then the LORD will scatter you among all peoples, from one end of the earth to the other, and there you shall serve other gods, which neither you nor your fathers have known—wood and stone. [65] And among those nations you shall find no rest, nor shall the sole of your foot have a resting place; but there the LORD will give you a trembling heart, failing eyes, and anguish of soul. [66] Your life shall hang in doubt before you; you shall fear day and night, and have no assurance of life. [67] In the morning you shall say, 'Oh, that it were evening!' And at evening you shall say, 'Oh, that it were morning!' because of the fear which terrifies your heart, and because of the sight which your eyes see.

[68] "And the LORD will take you back to Egypt in ships, by the way of which I said to you, 'You shall never see it again.' And there you shall be offered for sale to your enemies as male and female slaves, but no one will buy *you*."

Exhibit A: Clauses to aforementioned Contract with Satan

Words, thoughts and actions make and break contracts with Satan. I chose to disobey God and to believe the lies of Satan. I plan on "doing my own thing," because I know best. Therefore, I am aligned against God and against myself and against my body. I agree to take the curses for disobedience upon myself and my generations, as stated in Deuteronomy 28. Let the rebellion continue!

List **strongholds** that I continue to agree with by my words, thoughts and actions, i.e., Spirits of Bitterness, Self-Bitterness, Fear, Anxiety, Rejection, Unloving, Occult, Trauma, Envy and Jealousy, Unbelief, Soul Ties, Generational Curses, etc. List them here.	Because **I don't believe God** and I do believe the lies of Satan, I am signing up for the following curses. I do not agree to receive any blessings, but rather, I acknowledge and receive the curses, as mentioned in Deuteronomy 28. List them here.

Contract Payment Terms: <u>I pay all day, every day with all that I have, including my health.</u>

Signature: _____ Date: _____

Physiological Fruits of Sin
(Disease List)

PHYSIOLOGICAL FRUITS OF SIN — MASTER LIST

Diseases and their Spiritual and Emotional Strongholds

- ❖ **Acne:** Fear, anxiety, insecurity, depression and low self-esteem.
- ❖ **Acquired Immune Deficiency Syndrome (AIDS):** Anxiety, fear, fornication/uncleanness, rebellion and addictions.
- ❖ **Addictions/Addictive Personality:** Anxiety, fear, insecurity, depression, low self-esteem and unforgiveness.
- ❖ **Addison's Disease:** Self-hatred and guilt
- ❖ **Alzheimer's Disease:** Self-hatred, guilt, loss of identity, depression and anxiety.
- ❖ **Amyloidosis:** Broken heart, rejection, bitterness and self-rejection.
- ❖ **Amyotrophic Lateral Sclerosis (ALS or Lou Gehrig's Disease):** Fear, anxiety, self-hatred, self-rejection and occultism.
- ❖ **Ankylosing Spondylitis:** Inherited rejection, self-hatred, guilt and pain
- ❖ **Aplastic Anemia:** Broken heart, rejection/abandonment (usually by the father), self-rejection and guilt.
- ❖ **Arthritis:** Self-hatred, anger, anxiety and fear.
- ❖ **Asperger's Syndrome:** Inherited deaf and dumb spirit, matriarchal control, depression, self-rejection and occultism.
- ❖ **Asthma:** Inherited abandonment, rejection, worry and fear.
- ❖ **Astrocytoma:** Inherited bitterness or unforgiveness, self-bitterness and occultism.
- ❖ **Attention Deficit Disorder (ADD)/Attention Deficit Hyperactivity Disorder (ADHD):** Inherited confusion, anger, rejection, fear, abandonment, matriarchal control, rebellion, self-rejection and low self-esteem.
- ❖ **Autism:** Inherited deaf and dumb spirit (coming out of matriarchal control), rebellion and self-rejection.
- ❖ **Bacterial Meningitis:** Inherited anxiety, fear, rejection and abandonment.
- ❖ **Behcet's Syndrome:** Self-hatred, guilt, fear and loss of identity.
- ❖ **Bell's Palsy:** Anxiety, worry, fear, self-hatred and occultism.
- ❖ **Benign Prostatic Hyperplasia (Enlarged Prostate):** Self-bitterness, fornication, performance, anxiety and worry.
- ❖ **Berger's Disease (IgA Nephropathy):** Self-hatred, guilt and unforgiveness.
- ❖ **Bipolar Mood Disorder (Manic-Depression):** Depression, anger, anxiety and lack of discernment.
- ❖ **Bursitis:** Anxiety, fear, worry, self-bitterness and injury.
- ❖ **Cancers:**
    - ○ <u>Bladder Cancer:</u> Fear, anxiety, addictions and unforgiveness.
    - ○ <u>Bone Cancer (Osteosarcoma):</u> Inherited broken heart, bitterness, abandonment and fear.
    - ○ <u>Breast Cancer:</u> Bitterness (often toward female relatives), anxiety and fear.
    - ○ <u>Burkitt's Lymphoma:</u> Inherited rejection (usually from father), bitterness, fear of rejection and abandonment.

Adapted from: In His Own Image © 2003, by Art Mathias

- Chronic Myeloid Leukemia: Rejection (usually father), broken heart, bitterness, self-rejection, depression, anxiety.
- Cervical Cancer: Fornication, adultery, lack of self-esteem, infirmity and bitterness.
- Colon Cancer: Bitterness, anger, slander, accusation and fear.
- Hodgkin's Disease: Rejection (often by father), broken heart, bitterness, performance and drivenness.
- Leukemia: Rejection (usually father), broken heart, bitterness, self-bitterness and self-rejection.
- Liver Cancer: Bitterness, infirmity and addictions.
- Lung Cancer: Bitterness, addictions, anxiety and fear.
- Multiple Myeloma: Broken heart (from rejection), bitterness, self-rejection, fear, anxiety and depression.
- Non-Hodgkin's Lymphoma: Self-bitterness, rejection (often from father), anxiety, bitterness, self-rejection, guilt, fear of rejection and depression.
- Ovarian Cancer: Bitterness (due to absence of positive fathering), self-rejection (of her sexuality) and self-hatred.
- Pancreatic Cancer: Bitterness, self-bitterness, addictions, fear and anxiety.
- Prostate Cancer: Bitterness/unforgiveness (often toward male relatives), fornication and fear.
- Skin Cancer: Bitterness and self-neglect (not taking proper care of one's temple).
- Uterine Cancer: Bitterness, self-bitterness and fear.
- Waldenstrom's Macroglobulinemia: Self-bitterness, broken heart, bitterness, confusion and fear.

❖ **Candidiasis:** Broken heart, anxiety, worry, infirmity and bitterness.
❖ **Carpal Tunnel Syndrome:** Anxiety, fear, drivenness, self-hatred and depression.
❖ **Celiac Disease:** Inherited fear, anxiety, self-hatred and guilt.
❖ **Chronic Ear Infections:** Inherited fear of abandonment, rejection, fear, insecurity and infirmity.
❖ **Chronic Fatigue:** Self-hatred, anxiety, drivenness, performance, low self-esteem, guilt and depression.
❖ **Chronic Pain Syndromes:**
- Chronic Back Pain: Anxiety, worry, fear, anger, drivenness and bitterness.
- Chronic Pelvic Pain: Anger, bitterness (at the perpetrator), shame, guilt, regret, sorrow (directed at self) and depression.
- Psychogenic: Hatred, unforgiveness, depression, unhealthy introspection, oppression and self-pity.

❖ **Chronic Obstructive Pulmonary Disease (COPD):** Self-hatred, anxiety, fear, lack of trust in God and addictions.
❖ **Colic:** Fear of abandonment, rejection, fear, trauma and insecurity.
❖ **Costochondritis:** Anxiety, fear, insecurity and depression.
❖ **CREST Syndrome:** Self-hatred, hardness of heart, guilt and fear.

Adapted from: In His Own Image © 2003, by Art Mathias

- ❖ **Crohn's Disease:** Rejection, self-rejection, self-hatred, codependency, false burden bearing and guilt.
- ❖ **Cushing's Disease:** Fear, anxiety, victimization, self-hatred, guilt and depression.
- ❖ **Cystitis:** Fear, anxiety, self-hatred, infirmity and uncleanness.
- ❖ **Cysts:** Anxiety, fear and self-bitterness.
- ❖ **Deep Vein Thrombosis:** Anger and rage
- ❖ **Degenerative Disc Disease:** Anxiety, fear, addiction and depression.
- ❖ **Dementia:** Anxiety, fear and self-bitterness.
- ❖ **Depression (Unipolar):** Self-bitterness, self-condemnation, guilt, anxiety, hopelessness, danger, rage and hostility
- ❖ **Dermatitis:** Fear, anxiety and insecurity.
- ❖ **Diabetes:** Rejection (often from father), self-rejection, self-hatred, guilt, anxiety, fear and depression.
- ❖ **Diffuse Idiopathic Skeletal Hyperostosis (DISH):** Self-bitterness, self-hatred, guilt and fear.
- ❖ **Dissociative Disorder (DID) or Multiple Personality Disorder (MPD):** Fear, trauma and grief.
- ❖ **Diverticulitis:** Anxiety, fear and anger.
- ❖ **Dyslexia:** Inherited fear, insecurity, rebellion, rejection and abandonment.
- ❖ **Dysmenorrhea (Menstrual Cramps):** Self-hatred, bitterness, victimization, pain, fear anxiety and self-neglect.
- ❖ **Ear Infections (Chronic):** Inherited fear of abandonment, rejection, fear insecurity and infirmity
- ❖ **Eating Disorders:**
  - ○ <u>Anorexia Nervosa</u>: Self-hatred, low self-esteem, depression, denial, anger, addictions and insecurity
  - ○ <u>Bulimia Nervosa</u>: Self-hatred, low self-esteem, depression, denial, anger, addictions and insecurity.
  - ○ <u>Obesity</u>: Anxiety, fear, abandonment, emptiness, rage (from abuse – often sexual), depression, self-bitterness and low self-esteem.
- ❖ **Eclampsia:** Fear of abandonment, anger and self-hatred.
- ❖ **Endocarditis (Non-Bacterial):** Self-hatred and guilt.
- ❖ **Endometriosis:** Self-hatred, guilt, victimization and insecurity.
- ❖ **Environmental Illness (EI):** Fear, anxiety, broken heart, unhealthy introspection, self-hatred and self-pity.
- ❖ **Epilepsy (Idiopathic):** Deaf and dumb spirit, guilt and occultism.
- ❖ **Erectile Dysfunction (ED):** Fear, anxiety, self-hatred, depression, guilt and anger.
- ❖ **Essential Tremor:** Fear, anxiety, self-hatred and occultism.
- ❖ **Fibrocystic Breast Syndrome:** Self-bitterness, resentment (toward females in the family).
- ❖ **Fibromyalgic Syndrome:** Anxiety, fear, trauma, self-hatred, depression and drivenness.
- ❖ **Flesh-eating Bacteria (Necrotizing Fasciitis):** Anxiety, fear, insecurity, infirmity and occultism.
- ❖ **Frigidity (Female loss of sexual drive):** Anxiety, fear, depression, victimization and guilt.
- ❖ **Fungal Infections (Chronic):** Fear, anxiety, bitterness and infirmity.
- ❖ **Gallbladder Disease:** Bitterness, self-bitterness and fear.

Adapted from: In His Own Image © 2003, by Art Mathias

- ❖ **Gastritis:** Fear, anxiety, self-hatred, lack of trust in God, addictions and insecurity.
- ❖ **Gingivitis:** Anxiety, fear and self-hatred.
- ❖ **Glomerulonephritis:** Fear, anxiety, insecurity and self-anger.
- ❖ **Gout:** Self-bitterness, guilt, addictions (alcohol and food).
- ❖ **Grave's Disease (Hyperthyroid Disease):** Anxiety, fear, self-hatred and guilt.
- ❖ **Guillain-Barre Syndrome:** Anxiety, fear, insecurity and self-hatred.
- ❖ **Hair Loss:** Fear, anxiety, trauma and self-hatred.
- ❖ **Hashimoto's Disease (Hypothyroidism):** Self-hatred, guilt, fear and anxiety.
- ❖ **Headache Disorders:**
  - o <u>Tension-type Headaches:</u> Anxiety, fear, bitterness, worry, frustration and other negative emotions.
  - o <u>Migraine Headaches:</u> Guilt, anxiety, fear, self-conflict, pain and depression.
  - o <u>Rebound Headaches:</u> Dependence on drugs, anxiety, fear and other negative emotions.
- ❖ **Hearing Loss:** Anxiety, fear, infirmity, trauma, deaf and dumb spirit.
- ❖ **Heart Disease — Coronary Heart Disease (CHD):**
  - o <u>Atrial Fibrillation (A-FIB):</u> Fear of man, anxiety, fear, performance, self-hatred, hostility, bitterness, type-A behavior and depression.
  - o <u>Angina:</u> Fear, anxiety, anger, depression, bitterness and hostility.
  - o <u>Barlow's Syndrome (Billowing Mitral Valve Prolapse):</u> Fear, anxiety, anger, hostility and depression.
  - o <u>Cardiomyopathy:</u> Self-hatred, fear, anxiety, anger, hostility, depression and addictions.
  - o <u>Congestive Heart Failure:</u> Fear, anxiety, anger, self-bitterness, hostility and depression.
  - o <u>Coronary Artery Disease (CAD):</u> Self-anger, anger, rage, anxiety, fear, hostility, type-A behavior and depression.
- ❖ **Hepatitis (Chronic Active Hepatitis):** Infirmity, uncleanness, self-hatred, addictions, anxiety, fear.
- ❖ **Hernia:** Anger, rage.
- ❖ **Herpes Simplex Virus (HSV):**
  - o <u>HSV (Type 1) – Cold Sores or Fever Blisters:</u> Anxiety, fear, bitterness and self-hatred.
  - o <u>Genital Herpes (Type 2):</u> Anxiety, fear, bitterness, self-hatred, uncleanness and fornication.
  - o <u>Cytomegalovirus (CMV):</u> Anxiety, fear, bitterness, self-hatred, uncleanness and fornication.
  - o <u>Shingles:</u> Anxiety and fear.
  - o <u>Epstein-Barr Virus (Infectious Mononucleosis or Kissing Disease):</u> Anxiety, fear, bitterness, self-hatred and uncleanness.
- ❖ **High Blood Pressure (Essential Hypertension):** Fear, anxiety, anger and bitterness.
- ❖ **High Cholesterol (Familial Hypercholesteremia):** Self-anger, guilt, anxiety and fear.
- ❖ **Hives:** Fear and anxiety.
- ❖ **Hyperparathyroidism:** Fear, anxiety, self-bitterness and depression.
- ❖ **Hypoglycemic Syndrome:** Self-bitterness, anxiety, fear, fear of abandonment and lack of trust in God.

Adapted from: In His Own Image © 2003, by Art Mathias

- ❖ **Immunologic Idiopathic Thrombocytopenia Purpura:** Broken heart, rejection, self-rejection, self-hatred, guilt and fear of rejection.
- ❖ **Infertility:** Fear, anxiety, addictions, fornication, self-hatred, guilt and depression.
- ❖ **Insomnia and Night Terrors:** Fear, anxiety, depression, unforgiveness, occultism and lack of trust in God.
- ❖ **Insulin Resistance Syndrome:** Fear, self-rejection, self-anger and depression.
- ❖ **Interstitial Cystitis (IC):** Self-bitterness, guilt and insecurity.
- ❖ **Intercranial Hemorrhage:** Anger, fear, anxiety and rage.
- ❖ **Iritis:** Anxiety, fear, self-hatred, guilt and critical spirit.
- ❖ **Irritable Bowel Syndrome (IBS):** Anxiety, fear, unforgiveness, bitterness, trauma and depression.
  - o <u>Recurrent Abdominal Pain in Children:</u> Anxiety, fear (particularly of abandonment), fear of rejection and insecurity.
- ❖ **Kidney Stones:** Self-bitterness, self-rejection, anxiety and fear.
- ❖ **Lactose Intolerance:** Inherited rejection, fear of rejection and abandonment, and bitterness.
- ❖ **Leaky Gut Syndrome:** Self-hatred, fear, anxiety and unbelief (i.e., pharmakeia, dependence on drugs).
- ❖ **Lewy Body Disease:** Fear, self-hatred, guilt and occultism.
- ❖ **Lichen Planus:** Bitterness, self-hatred, guilt.
- ❖ **Lupus:** Self-hatred, self-conflict, guilt and performance.
- ❖ **Lyme Disease:** Fear, anxiety, self-hatred and guilt.
- ❖ **Malabsorption:** Fear and anxiety.
- ❖ **Masturbation:** Childhood fear and tension, uncleanness (inherited or learned), guilt and abuse.
- ❖ **Memory Loss:** Fear, anxiety, worry and severe trauma.
- ❖ **Menière's Disease:** Fear, anxiety, self-hatred and occultism.
- ❖ **Menopause (Aggravated):** Fear, anxiety, worry, resentment (of being female), fear of aging, abandonment, self-hatred, guilt and self-condemnation.
- ❖ **Menorrhagia (Heavy Uterine Bleeding):** Anxiety, fear, self-conflict about female issues, performance, addictions and guilt.
- ❖ **Miscarriage (recurrent) or Recurrent Spontaneous Abortion (RSA):** Self-hatred, bitterness, resentment (of being pregnant), hatred (toward the baby) and guilt.
- ❖ **Mixed Connective Tissue Disease:** Severe self-hatred, bitterness, resentment and guilt.
- ❖ **Multiple Sclerosis:** Rejection (often by father), self-hatred, guilt and depression.
- ❖ **Myasthenia Gravis:** Self-bitterness, guilt, grief, fear and anxiety.
- ❖ **Narcolepsy:** Anxiety, fear, self-bitterness, occultism (Freemasonry), and deaf and dumb spirit.
- ❖ **Osteoporosis:** Anxiety, fear, envy, self-bitterness, low self-esteem and depression.
- ❖ **Pancreatitis (chronic):** Addictions, self-bitterness, pride and insecurity.
- ❖ **Parasites:** Fear, anxiety and other negative emotions or thoughts.
- ❖ **Parkinson's Syndrome:** Inherited rejection (often from father), fear of rejection, occultism and hopelessness.
- ❖ **Pericarditis (Idiopathic):** Anxiety, fear of failure, self-hatred and guilt.

Adapted from: In His Own Image © 2003, by Art Mathias

- ❖ **Phobic or Fear and Anxiety Disorders:** Unbelief, fear, anxiety, trauma, worry, self-hatred, depression, guilt and shame.
    - o <u>Generalized Anxiety Disorder</u>
    - o <u>Panic Disorders or Panic Attacks</u>
    - o <u>Phobias</u>
    - o <u>Obsessive-Compulsive Disorder (OCD)</u>
    - o <u>Body Dysmorphic Disorder</u>
    - o <u>Trichtillomania</u>
    - o <u>Tourette's Syndrome</u>
    - o <u>Obsessive-Compulsive Personality (OCP)</u>
    - o <u>Post-Traumatic Stress Disorder (PTSD)</u>
    - o <u>Acute Stress Disorder</u>
- ❖ **Polycystic Ovarian Syndrome:** Fear, victimization, self-conflict, guilt and low self-esteem.
- ❖ **Post-Lyme Disease Syndrome:** Fear, doubt, unbelief and self-hatred.
- ❖ **Postpartum Depression:** Anxiety, fear, insecurity, self-hatred, shame, guilt and depression.
- ❖ **Preeclampsia:** Fear or conflict (with being female, being pregnant, or over the baby), anxiety, fear of abandonment, depression, self-bitterness, anger and guilt.
- ❖ **Premenstrual Syndrome (PMS):** Conflict (with being female), anger with God (for how he made the female body to function), anxiety, fear of abandonment, depression, self-bitterness, anger and guilt.
- ❖ **Psoriasis:** Self-hatred, guilt and fear of abandonment.
- ❖ **Pulmonary Fibrosis (Idiopathic):** Insecurity, self-rejection and self-hatred.
- ❖ **Reflex Sympathetic Dystrophy (RSD):** Self-bitterness, oppression, hatred, self-pity, fear of pain.
- ❖ **Reflux (Acid Reflux Disease):** Anxiety and fear.
- ❖ **Reiter's Syndrome:** Inherited self-hatred, guilt, self-accusation and insecurity, low self-esteem.
- ❖ **Resting Tremor:** Fear and anxiety.
- ❖ **Restless Leg Syndrome:** Fear, anxiety, oppression, self-bitterness and guilt.
- ❖ **Rosacea:** Anxiety, fear, anger and insecurity.
- ❖ **Sarcoidosis:** Broken heart, self-hatred, self-bitterness and fear of abandonment.
- ❖ **Schizophrenia:** Self-hatred, rejection, double-mindedness, insanity and confusion (from deaf and dumb spirit), rebellion, fear, inability to discern good from evil, depression and trauma.
- ❖ **Scleroderma:** Self-hatred, guilt and unforgiveness.
- ❖ **Scoliosis (Idiopathic):** Inherited self-conflict, anger, fear and rebellion — resulting in muscle-tension on one side of the back, causing an imbalance in the vertebrae.
- ❖ **Shingles (see Herpes)**
- ❖ **Sinusitis (Chronic):** Fear, anxiety, self-hatred and insecurity.
- ❖ **Sjogren's Syndrome:** Self-hatred, guilt and grief.
- ❖ **Sleep Apnea:** Self-hatred, fear and occultism.
- ❖ **Stevens-Johnson Syndrome:** Self-hatred, guilt, bitterness and accusation.
- ❖ **Strabismus:** Inherited self-hatred, occultism, double mindedness, and deaf and dumb spirit.

Adapted from: In His Own Image © 2003, by Art Mathias

- ❖ **Stroke:** Anger, rage and self-bitterness.
- ❖ **Stuttering:** Self-hatred, insecurity, fear of failure and a focus on performance.
- ❖ **Suicide:** Extreme self-hatred, self-bitterness, hopelessness and depression.
- ❖ **Synovitis:** Self-hatred, guilt and fear.
- ❖ **Tinnitus:** Anxiety, fear, occultism, and deaf and dumb spirit.
- ❖ **Transient Ischemic Attacks (TIAS):** Anxiety, fear, self-bitterness, performance and anger.
- ❖ **Trigeminal Neuralgia (Tic Douloureux):** Anxiety, fear, self-hatred, anger, pain and oppression.
- ❖ **Upper Respiratory Illness (URI):** Anxiety, fear, anger, self-bitterness, insecurity, frustration and any other negative emotions.
- ❖ **Ulcers:** Anxiety, fear, self-bitterness and insecurity.
- ❖ **Ulcerative Colitis:** Anxiety, self-bitterness and insecurity.
- ❖ **Uterine Fibroids:** Self-bitterness and fear of abandonment.
- ❖ **Varicose Veins:** Anger, self-anger.
- ❖ **Vitiligo:** Self-hatred, guilt, anxiety and fear.
- ❖ **Vulvodynia:** Fear, trauma, unforgiveness and fornication.
- ❖ **Wegener's Granulomatosis:** Self-anger, perfectionism and insecurity.
- ❖ **Wilson's Syndrome:** Anxiety, fear, abuse and depression.

Adapted from: In His Own Image © 2003, by Art Mathias

Made in United States
Orlando, FL
15 November 2024

53929889R10024